Are you Fierce, Focused & Fabulous or Just Another DUMB BITCH?

Are you Fierce, Focused & Fabulous or Just Another DUMB BITCH?

By: MsSoSick

Copyright 2010 MsSoSick
ISBN 978-0-557-51256-0

Acknowledgements

First and foremost I want to thank my one true God for blessing me with such creative talents! He is my, everything and without him, nothing else would be possible. And for this I give him thanks!

    I want to thank my Mom (Silvia Fisher) and Dad (Clyde Holliday) for without either of them there would be no me. I have to thank my inspiration and motivation, my Daughter the LOVE OF MY LIFE (Jade Deneé). I want to thank my Husband (Anthony Belser) for his love, continued support, and friendship. I want to thank my Sister (Melinda Holliday McDonald) for her constant advice and sisterly words of wisdom. My Nephew (Jaxon McDonald) and My God-Daughters (Mark-Asia Flint and Ariyana I want to thank my Best Friend/Soul Sister/ The God Mother of, my child Pinky (Mary Brown) she's helped me through it all and we've been through it all and she's most certainly My True Blue, LOVE YOU! I want to thank my Abuelita (R.I.P. Sarah Fisher) for always believing in me and wanting better for me. She was a Saint by any standards and yet she never judged me LOVE & MISS YOU DEARLY! I want to give a special thank you and shout out to Dimitri (Dim) Rey, Duret (Geo) McGough, and DJ 350, you three gentlemen really set me on my way! I also want to thank Brittany Davis my Graphic Designer, David Speer my Web Designer, Marc Bushelle my Photographer, Heith Chanel my Make-up Artist, Honey Cosmetics of Brooklyn, NY, Simon Duncan my Fashion Designer, Kelly J. Cadle my Stylist, my cousin Amanda Villacis, Tiffany Hasbourne aka Tiff The Stylist, DJ Ominaya of DA Union, Stephon Reed (Young Yacht Owners), Karl (Rage) Ferguson, Mr. Swagnificent aka Shawn Miller, and King Keino. I also want to thank Mello Soul (album coming soon) and Granny aka Mahalia Crump my Daughters Paternal Great Grand-Mother for their continued support during trying times. I LOVE YOU!

    I want to give a special thank you and acknowledgement to; DJ Johnny Han$um of DA Union, Miss Alecia (Leese) Lynshue, DJ Commish, and DJ Boof; my co-hosts/djs/and friends, for making BITCH ABOUT IT WITH MsSoSick possible and for being all around great and wonderful people. I LOVE YOU! And I have to give DJ Boof a special thank you and shout out for donating his time and handsome face to me, for free, by agreeing to be featured on the cover of this book, at the last minute! LOVE YOU! I also want to give a special shout out and thank you to my DTF RADIO Family; AR, Mark, Gage, Stan, Renny, Yobi, Mr. Radio, and the entire crew and cast LOL there are way too many of you to name, but thank you all!

I want to give the following people shout outs of acknowledgement for various reasons; DJ Profile aka Sean A. Malcolm, Manny Fresh, Lucky Don, Julito McCullum, Angela Yee, Shelina Parker, Ayesha Marks, Moe Sinatra, and Steven Hall (My West Coast Brother from Another). Thank you all!

I have to give a special shout out and thank you to My Dream Team; Paul Maxwell my Manager (84 Talent Management) and Tueré Rodriguez my Publicist aka The Celebrity Event Specialist.

And last but most certainly not least, I want and have to give a special shout and thank you to you; my readers, listeners, fans, and supporters. I thank you, because without your continued support NONE of this would be possible! I am forever thankful and grateful to you! I saved the best for last because you're all TheBomb.com!!

Kisses,
MsSoSick

PS

I almost forgot; I have to give a very special thank you and shout out to all the Dumb Bitches of the world, because you are truly the reason and inspiration behind this book! LOL

Table of Contents

Prologue 9
Chapter 1. Its 2010 WELFARE is NOT a Career! 1
Chapter 2. Stop living vicariously through your Child/ren.........5
Chapter 3. Are you his "Woman" or his "Sideline Hoe"?..........9
Chapter 4. Low Self-Esteem/Desperation is NOT cute you DUMB BITCH it's a Killer..15
Chapter 5. STOP lowering the bar you DUMB BITCH 21
Chapter 6. DUMB BITCHES with fucked up ass priorities..............23
Chapter 7. DUMB BITCHES that fall victim to Domestic Violence..25
Chapter 8. Ungrateful ass MEN!...29
Chapter 9. Self-Hating DUMB BITCHES.................................31
Chapter 10. My Two Cents on DUMB BITCHES who INSIST on Having "Keep a Nigga" Babies..............................33
Chapter 11. DUMB BITCHES that insist on fucking for FREE 35
Chapter 12. He is your son/brother/cousin/baby-daddy/friend NOT YOUR MAN 39
Chapter 13. DUMB BITCHES that "THINK" they're hot when they're NOT 41
Chapter 14. Act your age you DUMB BITCH Feigning a mid-life crisis isn't Cute..43
Chapter 15. DUMB BITCHES that would much rather take care of a man instead of their child/ren...........................45
Chapter 16. They're either Haters or Band Wagon Jumpers 47
Chapter 17. DUMB BITCHES The Recession and The "American" Dream..49
Chapter 18. Ode to Winter 51
Chapter 19. (Epilogue) In The End 53

Prologue

First let me start by saying that the purpose of this book is not to tare women and or men down, but, to EMPOWER them. Its purpose is to give women and men a chance to step back and re-evaluate any situation that they may be in, where they are conducting themselves like a DUMB BITCH! Please be advised that the word BITCH in my world DOES NOT pertain to any one specific sex but both sexes!

Everyone has played the DUMB BITCH role at some point in their life, including myself, so let's get that straight from the gate! However, not all of us have been able to accept the fact that we're caught up in a DUMB BITCH situation, get out of it, and rise above it. Some of us just stay in it, and apparently bask in the ambiance of being a DUMB BITCH, as if it were a good thing.

In any event, I have decided to single handedly start a movement to bring the reign of the DUMB BITCH to an end!

I want all of my real women and men living life FABULOUSLY, to stand up join hands, and take this journey with me. This road is not an easy one to travel, but it's one we must take. So, get ready for the ride, because it's going to be a rocky one!

I am so sick of that DUMB BITCH is the name of movement, and if you aren't up on it yet, YOU DAMN WELL SHOULD BE!

Welcome to the life and times of MsSoSick the realest Bitch you know and definitely the realest Bitch you will ever meet!

Chapter 1

Its 2010 WELFARE is NOT a Career!

I decided to start with DUMB BITCHES that view getting on welfare, staying on welfare, and manipulating the system for as long as possible, as some sort of career move. Only because, these ignorant, lazy ass DUMB BITCHES get under my damn skin! I hate fucking losers! And yeah, if what I stated above applies to you or describes you, then that makes you a FUCKING LOSER!

WELFARE is NOT a come up YOU DUMB BITCH! How can you possibly believe that you have a chance of achieving Fierce, Focused, Fabulosity by making a career out of being on welfare? Please explain it to me, because seriously, I just don't get it!

Welfare should be a means to an end, NOT the end all and be all! Please understand this NOW, and I mean RIGHT NOW!

I am not knocking anyone on welfare. I understand that EVERYONE including myself can be susceptible to falling on hard times. However, I think welfare should be used as a vehicle to get you up and out of those times. Not something that you should ever be complacent, and satisfied with or something you should continuously rely upon! The world is your oyster and the income provided to you through welfare can't even get you a fraction of that oyster. Life is not a dress rehearsal; you only get one chance, MAKE THE BEST OF IT!

If you are on welfare, and have been on welfare for more than four years, and you are not enrolled in any form of higher education program, and have no intentions of ever enrolling in some sort of higher education program, then you are a DUMB BITCH! If instead of waking up one day and saying, "You know what, welfare isn't enough anymore. I need to get up, get out, and get something". You say "Damn I need to have me another baby so that I can get an increase in my benefits"! You're a DUMB BITCH! You are pathetic, disgusting, repulsive, and lazy! You are the reason our economy is as fucked up as it is! You are the reason, when a REAL WOMAN applies for benefits because she has fallen on hard times, she is put through a ringer to get them! Even though she, unlike you has actually contributed to the pot that these funds are distributed from, because unlike you she is a PRODUCTIVE member of society, where you are just a leech! You are the epitome of what makes a DUMB BITCH a DUMB BITCH! You are dumb, ignorant, lazy, and frankly a waste of fucking space!

Lucky for you, MsSoSick is here to help!

If you're on welfare and you have been for the past four years, and like I said, are not enrolled in some sort of higher education program, I want you to change that IMMEDIATELY! If you can't enroll in a higher education program, because you still haven't completed your secondary education (High School) then what I want you to do is get up, find a GED course, and enroll yourself immediately!

I know that some of you may feel embarrassed about what your friends and family will say; well I'm here to tell you, FUCK THEM! This is your life, and yes while you may not have made much of it, you can still change that! You can still become the Fierce, Focused, & Fabulous woman you were born to be! It's NEVER too late! No one is perfect, hell, I'm NOT perfect, so don't allow others to judge you and make you feel like you can't be or do anything with your life, because you can!

Hell a black man is President of THE most powerful country in the world! That right there should tell you, I can do anything I want, I can be anything I want, and I don't have to be a DUMB, LAZY, IGNORANT, UNEDUCATED BITCH anymore!

Aren't you sick and tired of having to go down to the HRA office to explain your situation over and over again? To some case worker none the less that looks down on you like a piece of shit? Aren't you embarrassed to be working for the Parks Department picking up trash because that's all society thinks someone of your caliber is capable of doing? How can you not be embarrassed, is what I want to know? I see you, looking HOT as hell in that summer heat with your little stick with the knife on the end, picking up stray paper and what not, looking miserable as shit! Does it really make sense to work that hard, for what I'm sure equates to even less than minimum wage? Don't you think it would make more sense to get an education, and get yourself a job, where you can hold your head up high? Where you can look forward to receiving a Christmas or performance bonus, attend office parties, and have an opportunity to meet someone Fabulous that you can look up to, and that can continue to motivate you to do better and want better for yourself? Don't you want your children to look at you with pride in their eyes? Don't you want to look yourself in the mirror and finally like the person you see looking back?

Let TODAY be the day you take your life back! Let TODAY be the day that you start to dream again! Let TODAY be the day you start to love you again! Let TODAY be the day that you look in the mirror and say, "You know what, I deserve better than this, I am better than this, I want better than this, I am going to do BETTER THAN THIS"! Today is YOUR DAY, so seize the moment Diva, Carpe Diem!

Chapter 2

Stop living vicariously through your Child/ren

These particular DUMB BITCHES get under my skin, but they get on my fucking nerves too!

Its one thing to say "Do as I say, not as I do" and it's an entirely separate thing to say "Do as I say, not as I do, even though everything I say is IGNORANT as shit"! If you have children and you are the kind of DUMB BITCH I talked about in Chapter 1, please stop trying to give your child/ren advice! Please STOP setting unreasonable and unrealistic goals for your children, when you are in no way capable of helping them achieve said goals! You are only doing your child/ren a disservice and setting the course for them to ultimately resent you! You are setting them up for failure; you are setting them up to end up like you! And, the world really does not need yet another addition to the DUMB BITCH team!

I'm not telling you that you shouldn't want a better life and or future for your children, because you should, all parents should! What I am telling you, is if your child comes home from school, and you never inquire as to how their day went, what homework assignments they have to complete, what projects if any they have to work on, or if they understand the material being taught; then you cannot beat, or chastise them when they fail! Your child/ren can only succeed if you show a constant interest in their lives! Beating your child/ren for not excelling in school, doing well, and or being ranked at the top of their class, especially when you aren't helping them get there, makes you a DUMB BITCH with misplaced anger issues! Stop abusing your child/ren because YOU are a failure! Stop setting unrealistic goals for your child/ren, and chastising them when they cannot accomplish them! How DARE you expect your child/ren to grow up and be the next President, General Surgeon, District Attorney, or world's Greatest

Entertainer, when you yourself can't even read? When you yourself can't even write? When you yourself can't even compose a decent English sentence? JUST STOP IT! Maybe if you would have done MORE with your pathetic excuse of a life, your child/ren would have a better chance at accomplishing all of the things that you wish for him/her. But since you've wasted your life and time, now you want to live vicariously through your child, now you want your child to be the HNIC (Head Nigga in Charge) because in an essence you are nobody! Life doesn't work like that! YOU have to set the building blocks for your child/ren, if you can't help your child/ren who can, who will? If you see your child struggling in school or in life you have to step in and find away to help them, and if you can't then you need to find someone who can! Find them a mentor. Maybe you have a relative, or friend that is doing well, that wouldn't mind taking your poor unfortunate offspring under their wing and providing them with some form of guidance (don't be ashamed to ask for help, be ashamed not to). But realize that they do NEED guidance! You beating on them, chastising the, telling them that they are not good enough, yet expecting them to be doctors when they grow up, because that's what you really wanted for yourself is NOT good enough! They need more than that and they deserve more than that from you!

If you are a fat, undesirable, and unattractive woman, stop forcing your daughter to compete in beauty contests! Stop calling her fat and ugly because that's how you feel about you! Stop telling her she needs to exercise and go on a diet, so that she can be the FABULOUS and thin DIVA you always wanted to be! STOP living vicariously through your child/ren. It's one thing to not feel good about yourself it's an entirely different thing to make your child/ren feel bad about who they are. Because, who they are is a direct reflection of whom you are. If you want a seed to flourish, and grow into a wonderful plant or tree some day, you have to water it NOT piss on it you DUMB BITCH! If you are a DUMB BITCH like the DUMB BITCH I defined in Chapter 1 (ignorant, pathetic, lazy) the chances of your child/ren being successful are nil to none. People in general first begin to covet (that means want for all you DUMB IGNORANT BITCHES reading this) what they see every day. This means, the chances of your child wanting to own a home after living in the projects their entire life, isn't likely. More likely than not, they will feel, as if they've lived there all their life, so has their mother, and her mother/father and they're doing just fine why should I move? Because children DEFINITELY covet what they see, because it's all they know! If you live in the projects and your children watch you bust your ass every day to get out, and make something better of your life, whether you ever do or don't is irrelevant. Because, they have seen you at the very least try! And believe me, when it's their turn, this is what they will say, "Damn I watched my mom bust her ass to provide a good life for me, I watched her do the best she could with what little she had, and now that I'm an adult I'm going to help make her dream come true! I'm going to study/work extra hard so that someday I can move my Mama up out of here. She may not know it yet, but I have plans for her, for us. I have plans to create a better life for us. Yeah, she may not have made it, but I'm going to make sure she sees that I've made it before she leaves this earth". People covet what they first see. If you want better, you have to do better. It can't start with your child/ren it has to start with you!

Even if you have to sit your child/ren down and say, "Look, Mama didn't make much of her life, but I'm going to see to it that you do better than me. I may not be able to help you, but tell me what you need and I will get it for you. If you need a mentor, a tutor whatever it may be, you tell me and I'm going to make sure you have it. Because, you succeeding, you being the best you that you can be, because you want to be is what's important. Don't do what I do, don't end up like me, you're better than this. Hell I'm better than this; I just realized it too late. I love you and I don't want you to make the same mistakes I've made. I want you to learn from them, and make better choices than I did, so when you have your own children you won't have to have this conversation. Let your life be an example to them, that even though you came from nothing, and you didn't have much, you rose above it and that dreams no matter how big or small do come true". This is what you need to tell your children, this is how you help your children. Positive energy, brings about a positive result, negative energy will undoubtedly bring about a negative result.

Your child/ren like you and I are human they are not perfect and in turn will make mistakes. Help them learn and grow for them, don't stick their noses in it! They're not fucking dogs you DUMB BITCH, they are your children! You had your chance and you wasted it, STOP trying to make their life your life, STOP trying to make their chance, your chance to get it right! STOP living vicariously through your child/ren. STOP being a controlling, and manipulative DUMB BITCH!

Chapter 3

Are you his "Woman" or his "Sideline Hoe"?

I absolutely hate it, when DUMB BITCHES are in denial about their situations! I hate it when DUMB BITCHES make up stories and fairy tales to make their relationships seem more appealing and desirable to others! I hate it when DUMB BITCHES not only lie to you, but lie to themselves about the role they play in their "mans" life! I just fucking hate it! If you're the "Sideline Hoe" you DUMB BITCH, accept it, deal with it, and or move the fuck on! Because lying about it, does not change a damn thing about it! Know that NOW, and I mean RIGHT NOW!

Don't you just hate it when some DUMB BITCH calls you up and says, yeah he's about to cop me (buy) so and so, or he's about to take me so and so, and you know damn well that this motherfucker hasn't even taken her lame DUMB BITCH ass to the fucking corner store before!?! Or am I the only one with that issue?

Don't you hate it when a DUMB BITCH can come up with a million excuses as to why she's NEVER been to her (let her tell it) "mans" house? But you and I know damn well that he isn't her man, at best he's her "Jump Off" and that's why her dumb ass hasn't ever been invited over! Or am I the only one with that issue?

** The ONLY exceptions to this rule are if a man is ashamed of where he lives, comes from, and or his family. Your FABULOUSNESS may be a little intimidating to him! However, this is rarely ever the case and I mean rare! If it is you will immediately know because it'll be blatantly OBVIOUS that you're just better off than him (more likely than not financially) and he's lucky to have captured your attention!

Don't you hate to hear a DUMB BITCH plan her entire life around and with a man that you know and she knows damn well doesn't give a fuck about her? Or is that just my issue?? Because let me tell you, that bullshit gets under my motherfucking skin!

Scenario Number One

Okay DUMB BITCHES, listen up, because this scenario is for you! If you are dealing with a dude you only get to see late at night, he is NOT your man! If you are dealing with a dude and he's getting money and watching you struggle he is NOT your man! If you're dealing with a dude that lives with another woman i.e. wife, ex-wife, girlfriend, ex-girlfriend, baby-mama (and I don't give a fuck what kind of excuse he gave you for his living arrangement) he is NOT your man! If you're dealing with a dude and he makes up an entire story/lie about how he's being deported, so that he doesn't have to see you anymore, he is NOT your man (in fact this motherfucker HATES YOU) Don't say I never warned you! If you didn't know it (the reason behind his living arrangements) was a lie originally, when you found out it was, you should have known then, that he was NOT your man, nor had he ever had intentions of becoming your man! If you get into a fight (verbal and or physical) with your Baby-Daddy's other Baby's-Mama, Girlfriend, and or Wife, and he jumps in (and it's NOT on your side), he is NOT your man! If you are messing with a dude, and he constantly cuts you off for months at a time, and comes back whenever he deems fit, he is NOT your man! If you have been dealing with a dude for over a year, and invite him to your child's birthday party and he is a no show (for whatever reason) he is NOT your man! If you have been dealing with a dude for over a year, and you are not invited to or allowed to participate in any of his child/rens milestones, he is NOT your man! If you have been dealing with a dude for over a year, and you have not been introduced to his child/ren, and he has taken no interest in meeting your child/ren, he is NOT your man! If you're dealing with a dude, and he's on the phone with you, and you hear a voice in the background ask, "Who's that, _____"? ****Fill in any name other than your own**; he is NOT your man! If you are dealing with a dude and he rarely if ever spends quality time with you, he is NOT your man! I don't care how busy a man is, he ALWAYS makes time for what is important to him! If you're dealing with a dude, for over three months, and you think the two of you are exclusive, yet you have no clue as to what his real name is, and or where he lives, he is NOT your man! If you're dealing with a dude for over three months, and you feel that you're situation is an exclusive one, yet when you run into him in the streets, he either A) Greets you as if you were just a friend (no kiss or warm embrace) and or B) Introduces you by name but with no title and or only uses the title FRIEND when introducing you, he is NOT your man! I don't care what bullshit, or lame ass line he feeds you after the fact, he is NOT your man! If you're dealing with a dude and he has to leave your house before the sun comes up for whatever reason, he is NOT your man! If you're dealing with a dude that has money, but you still have to call your friends and family to borrow money just to make ends meet, he is NOT your man! If you are dealing with a dude and he has designated a day of the week just for you, he is NOT your man, you are his _____ **Fill in the day of the week**! If you are dealing with a dude and you are the only one in the relationship giving 100% of yourself at all times, he is NOT your MAN! If you're dealing with a dude and every time he goes home he has to turn his phone off, he is NOT your man! If you are dealing with a dude, and his Baby-Mama (not their child/ren, just her) Mama, Sister, Aunt, Cousins, and of Female Friends needs come before yours, he is NOT your man (Because none of those women should be; feeding, clothing, cooking, and or fucking him) So all of them should have to fall the fuck back whenever you come calling! And, last but certainly not least, if your man is married, if your man has a legal wife, then he is NOT YOUR MAN, he is HER HUSBAND! Please do NOT get it twisted! You are his "Jump Off/Mistress/Whore" in other words you DUMB BITCH, you're nothing more than his "Sideline Hoe"! Deal with it, get over it, and or do something about it! But, whatever you do decide to do, please STOP being a DUMB BITCH about it!

Let me explain something to you about a real man, because I have one! When a man is your man, you don't need to lie and make up stories of grandeur. His actions alone and the manner in which he treats you will serve as a clear indication to all that not only is he YOUR MAN but YOU are HIS WOMAN!

Scenario Number Two

If your man has the means, and you need for something, and you don't even have to ask for it, but he automatically knows, and just handles it, then you have yourself a REAL MAN! A real man will never sit on the sidelines and watch his woman struggle. If your man has his own place, and you are constantly invited over for sleepovers, and movie night, you have yourself a REAL MAN! If a man has to choose between doing something important for you, his Baby-Mama, Mama, or any of the aforementioned women is "Scenario One", and choses your needs over theirs, he is indeed YOUR man, because your needs will and should ALWAYS come first. A real man knows that he can't take care of anything or anyone else until he has taken care of "home". His Baby-Mama is only his Baby-Mama, for a reason! And frankly if she's not calling for or about the child/ren she shouldn't be calling at all! Her needs and or wants as long as they do not concern their child/ren should NEVER EVER supersede your own, and if you have a REAL MAN they won't! His Mama is his mother, and yes she is responsible for his very life force, BUT unless she is crippled or in some other way incapacitated, should not have to constantly rely on her son to do every damn thing for her! If she does, when a situation like this arises he should be man enough to say "Mom I have to do something important for her first, (and, but, or) as soon as I'm done I can come and help you". Then again, his Mama could be a needy and lonely DUMB BITCH that he has allowed to become way too dependent on him; in that case a different approach is needed, and the manner in which he handles the situation will vary, this is no reflection of how he feels for you and has no bearing on your role in his life. I'll discuss that particular kind of DUMB BITCH in a later chapter entitled (He is your son/brother you DUMB BITCH not your man)! If your man likes to stay and have some morning sex, watch a TV show, and or the news, check out the weather, talk with you, and eat breakfast before he leaves the next morning, then you have yourself a REAL MAN! If you can call your man, any day of the week, with absolutely no notice and say "Hey Babe, I want to hang out today" or "Hey Babe, I want you to come over and spend the night with me tonight" in other words, if a man is your man every day is your day and any day can be your day, if you can do either of those two things, you have yourself a REAL MAN! Your man will not assign you any particular day of the week. He will enjoy spending time with you just as much as you enjoy spending time with him, no matter what day of the week it is. When you speak of your future and the future of your relationship, if your man, follows up with positive feedback, not if, ands, buts, or maybes, but "Yes baby that sounds great, I'm looking forward to it too" then you have yourself, a REAL MAN.

In conclusion…

If the first scenario I described best fits your relationship well then Darling I'm sorry to tell you, but that man is NOT YOUR MAN you are his "Jump Off/Sideline Hoe" at best! Now, if scenario number two, best describes your relationship, congratulations, you have yourself a REAL MAN!

For all of you DUMB BITCHES that can best identify with scenario #1, it gets worse, because you have allowed yourself to be played as his "Sideline Hoe" he will NEVER view you as anything else. You will NEVER be his woman, and most certainly you will NEVER EVER be his wife! Wake up, get a grip, and find a fucking clue you DUMB BITCH! That man doesn't want you! And, what he does want from you I'm sure he gets it when ever and where ever he wants it! Because let's face it if he wanted you to really be his woman you would've been by now. And yes, while he may say, "Baby, you know it's you I want, you know it's you I love, I'm just not that kind of man, to be all up on a woman and spending time with her and you know I ain't no trick" BITCH he is feeding you some weak lame ass game! But, because you're a DUMB BITCH you're swallowing the hell out of that teaspoon of Bullshit and sugar to help it go down. You're NOT the one sweetie. Now, he may not be with anyone else, he may not have a real girl, but know that, that does NOT make you it! You are what you are, and what you are, is a "Sideline Hoe" and an easily manipulated DUMB BITCH!

Remember, lying about it and denying it, will not change a damn thing. The only thing that can change the dynamics of your "make believe" relationship is you! And, to change it, you have to end it. There is no saving it, there is no trying to convince him that you are a good woman and should be the one. His mind is made up, and you are not it! Dump his ass, change your ways, get your mind right, money right, and get ready for war. Start living life in what I like to call "The Diva Lane" and that good man you want, will find you! But please be advised, that low-self esteem and settling for whatever some man offers you is not a good way to land the man of your dreams. The only type of man you can attract in that state of mind is a predator, and a real man is no predator, he is a provider and protector. So, if your man is neither provider or protector, but manipulator or predator, know these two things, he is NOT your man, he's not even a real man!

See you in "The Diva Lane"!

Chapter 4

Low Self-Esteem/Desperation is NOT cute you DUMB BITCH it's a Killer

I hate this topic, I hate the fact that I even need to address and speak on this topic. But, because so many of you DUMB BITCHES have fucked up Self-Esteem, I must.

Humans are animals, by nature. A very advanced animal, but we are animals none the less. All animals are born with innate senses. It's how we survive. And in the jungle we know, that only the strong survive. The weak; are killed, eaten, and or discarded. Either way, the weak is always destroyed. Know that weak = death!

When you suffer from Low Self-Esteem and or reek of desperation, the world views you as weak, and hence you are more susceptible to being preyed on and or attacked by predators (as mentioned in Chapter 3)!

In this case the predator that I'm referring to is some good for nothing motherfucker that is going to use the fact that you have low self-esteem and are desperate for attention and affection from a man against you! He is going to use you and drain you dry. When he is done with you, there will be even less of you left than there is now, and thoughts of suicide are sure to follow. DEATH!

Lucky for you MsSoSick is here to help! I'm going to help you get out of the funk that you're in, take your life back, and get that good for nothing motherfucker up out of your life for good! And because I can't stand a good for nothing motherfucker, I'm going to school you on how to get a little get back while you're at it!

Lesson 1

If you suffer from low self-esteem now is NOT a good time for you to look for a man, casually date, and or engage in random sexual encounters. Now is NOT the time for you to worry about your lack of a companion. Now is the time for some "Me Time"! Now is the time for some self-reflection. Start by asking yourself these simple questions: Why am I depressed? Why am I so hard on myself? Why do I not feel good about myself? and Why do I think I need a man to complete me? **If you're too ashamed to admit this is your reality, feel free to ask yourself these questions in your head or while alone. Also be sure to write down your answers. Sometimes seeing things in black and white make them a little more real.** Until, you can answer these questions and cope with them, you DO NOT need to think about getting into a relationship, dating, or engaging in any sort of random sexual encounters! If you cannot love yourself, how do you expect anyone else to love you? Maybe you need therapy, maybe you need a long vacation, maybe you need to pack your shit up and head cross country for a fresh start. But whatever you need, know that, it IS NOT A MAN!

Lesson 2

If you are suffering from low self-esteem because you have just gone through a traumatic break-up, and or divorce, I want you to get up and shake that shit off right now! Because I can assure you that where ever he is, you are not on his mind, he is not depressed, and his self-esteem in intact! The only one you are doing a disservice to, is yourself! Yes, break ups hurt, I can only imagine going through a divorce is worse, but you can NOT allow yourself to be defeated! Think of yourself as a Phoenix! Emerge from the ashes, push through the destruction and rise to the occasion! Get your hair done, get your nails done, have a spa day, call your girls and hit the clubs, lounges, bars or all three, let your hair down and enjoy your life. Because while your relationship may be over, your life isn't! Life goes on, whether you want it to or not. So don't let that motherfucker control you after all is said and done. Claim your life, your destiny, and your spirit back! You may not have him, but you still have you, and at the end of the day, that's what's most important! Stop being a DUMB BITCH and be a REAL BITCH, start living your life for you; Fierce, Focused, & FABULOUSLY!

Lesson 3

Desperation is NOT CUTE and predators can smell it a mile away! If you carry yourself like a desperate DUMB BITCH please be advised that you will be treated as such! You're worse than the DUMB

BITCH with low self-esteem and I'll tell you why, desperation is a conscious decision, while normally low self-esteem comes as an indirect result of suffering from some form of depression, whether it be recently onset or manic.

If you're not sure if you're a Desperate DUMB BITCH, please pay close attention, because I'm about to tell you!

If the minute, you meet a man, you begin to envision yourself walking down the aisle in that flowing white dress, then yes you're what I call, a Desperate DUMB BITCH. If you try to make every man you date your boyfriend, or view every man you date as a potential boyfriend, the yes you're what I call, a Desperate DUMB BITCH. If a man is showing you as little attention as possible, practically ignoring you and calling you a "Bug-a-Boo" yet you continue to refer to him as your "man", then yes you're what I call a Desperate DUMB BITCH. If when your man calls you're at his beck and call, because you fear the repercussions of not always being available when he needs you, then yes you're what I call a Desperate DUMB BITCH. If every time you go out with your friends you try and pin point your "mans" location so that you can see him, if only for 5 seconds, then yes you're a Desperate DUMB BITCH. If you allow a man to mistreat you, physically, and or verbally abuse you, and not only do you stay, but justify his treatment of you, then yes you're what I call an extremely STUPID & Desperate DUMB BITCH. If you own a car, but are forced to take the train, bus, and or a taxi because your "man" needs the car, then yes you're what I call a Desperate DUMB BITCH!

Now, there are quite a few different scenarios that can qualify you as a Desperate DUMB BITCH, the ones listed above are just to name a few. If you can identify with any of those, then yes you are what I call a Desperate DUMB BITCH. If you can't identify with any of these, but still think that there is a possibility that you are a Desperate DUMB BITCH, chances are, you are.

So take a moment, step back and re-evaluate your situation. If you have come to the conclusion that you are a Desperate DUMB BITCH, don't worry there is still time for you to change. Like I stated earlier, desperation is a conscious decision. I want you to consciously decide that you will no longer conduct yourself as the Desperate DUMB BITCH you used to be, you will no longer allow yourself to be treated as the Desperate DUMB BITCH you used to be, but as the Lady & REAL DIVA that you've come to be!

Live your life for you and make sure you live it; Fierce, Focused, & FABULOUSLY!

Now as far as some get back, this is what you do, this goes for both formerly depressed low self-esteem having DUMB BITCHES as well as formerly Desperate DUMB BITCHES. And the reason I'm telling you this is because PREDATORS need to know what it feels like to be preyed upon! KARMA IS A REAL BITCH MOTHERFUCKER!!

THIS IS WHERE YOU GET SOME GET BACK!

Depending on your situation, the best way to hurt a man is to USE him and DISCARD him! Now you can't do this and not get rid of him because this will put you right back into a DUMB BITCH situation. Tell him you need something, anything, EXPENSIVE CLOTHES, BAG, SHOES, YOUR RENT PAID, YOUR CAR NOTE PAID, YOUR MORTGAGE PAID, AN ALL EXPENSES PAID VACATION TO YOUR DREAM DESTINATION, like I said, something, anything (of substantial value)! If he is really worried about losing you he'll pay like the stupid fucking douche bag he is! But if he really thinks he got it like that, he WONT pay, however he will keep pressing to see you. DO NOT SEE HIM WITH OUT BEING COMPENSATED for your time, pain, and suffering (He owes you)! Tell him, unfortunately at this time you have NO TIME FOR LAME BITCH ASS NIGGAS and what he needs to do is LOSE YOUR FUCKING PHONE NUMBER, GET A GRIP, AND FIND A FUCKING CLUE!

If he is willing to compensate you, for your heart ache and time, TAKE THAT MOTHERFUCKER FOR EVERYTHING YOU CAN! Then hit him with the, "Sorry Boo, I have NO TIME FOR YOU! Because I'm a REAL BITCH & REAL BITCHES DO REAL THINGS! So kick rocks motherfucker, thanks for the gifts, and charge it to the game payback is a motherfucker like you"! Then laugh really obnoxiously into his ear and hang up on his ass! He may be ranting and raving calling you all sorts of names at this point or he may be sitting there speechless LOL either way it's not your problem HANG UP AND NEVER EVER TAKE HIS CALL OR ACKNOWLEDGE his presence again!

Enjoy your Get Back!!

I guarantee, that while he may never, ever have another kind word for you, he'll know that he got played like the DUMB BITCH ASS NIGGA that he really is! ONLY the sorry & pathetic prey on the weak and unfortunate so for this he deserves to feel PLAYED!

Always remember this, "NEVER ALLOW SOMEONE TO BECOME YOUR "PRIORITY" IF YOU'RE ONLY THEIR "OPTION" Author Unknown.

Good luck! Stay strong DIVA!

Chapter 5

STOP lowering the bar you DUMB BITCH

I want to talk about DUMB BITCHES that insist on lowering the bar because they have NO self-worth or they have NO CLUE as to what their worth is.

I'll tell you why I hate these particular DUMB ASS BITCHES. I hate them because, when a man that has dated one of them, prior to meeting and or dating a Real Bitch like me, he is caught completely off guard.

Because of that DUMB BITCH he's used to NOT having to do anything. He's used to being praised for being mediocre. I barely praise greatness! I don't give a fuck if you're a father to your children, YOU'RE SUPPOSED TO BE THAT DUMB ASS! I don't care if you pay the rent, mortgage, car note, etc. YOU'RE SUPPOSED TO PAY THAT DUMB ASS! I don't give a fuck if any man does what HE IS SUPPOSED TO DO as a man! Who the fuck praises me for doing what the fuck I'm supposed to do? NO ONE that's who!

But these pathetic ass bitches who aren't use to shit, praise these simple motherfuckers for everything! SO when they run up on a REAL BITCH like me, what's the 1st thing he says; "YOU'RE SPOILED, YOU WANT TOO MUCH, DAMN AM I SUPPOSED TO DO EVERYTHING, DAMN NIGGAS REALLY DO ALL OF THAT"? AHHH, YEAH MOTHERFUCKER THEY DO! It takes GREATNESS TO FUCK WITH GREATNESS! And I my dear friend AM FUCKING GREAT!

I hate bitches that aren't used to shit, so when a man takes her dumb ass through the drive thru she has to call and "brag"! I'm like damn, not only are you a DUMB BITCH but you're, PATHETIC and you're fucking up the game for REAL BITCHES like ME, living life "Fierce, Focused, & FABULOUSLY"! I hate these bitches; they get on my fucking nerves! And because they haven't figured out how to be a real bitch and live life in "The Diva Lane", what do they do? That's right, they HATE! That's all a DUMB BITCH like that can do anyway, is HATE! HATE on MY GREATNESS, MY FOCUS, MY FIERCENESS, & you know that Dumb Bitch is most certainly HATING ON MY FABULOSITY! STOP hating you DUMB BITCH and STEP YOUR MOTHERFUCKING UP GAME instead!

Here are some clues to let you know whether or not YOU NEED TO STEP YOUR GAME UP

1. If you tell your "man" that there is no food in your house, and he brings you over a #1 instead of taking you grocery shopping. You need to step up your game!

2. If you tell your "man" that your car broke down and needs fixing, and he asks you, when do you get paid? And you say "in two weeks", and he says, "oh that's not too bad, you'll be driving again before the month is over". You need to step up your game up!

3. If you tell your "man" "You want to catch a movie" and he asks, "What time does the matinee start tomorrow"? You need to step your game up!

4. If you tell your man, "let's catch a show and do dinner", and he takes you to a movie and McDonalds, you need to step your game up!

5. If you tell your man, "the rent is due, the cable bill is due, the phone bill is due, the electricity bill is due, the water bill is due, and the gas bill is due", and all he can say is, "well you better pay it soon". BITCH, you need to step your motherfucking game up!

All I can say is stop settling for less or little to nothing and remember a penis doesn't make him a man. His will to be and character does!

Chapter 6

DUMB BITCHES with fucked up ass priorities

This DUMB BITCH scenario applies to BOTH men and women.

I hate DUMB ASS BITCHES with fucked up ass priorities; let's get that clear right now.

BTW & FYI; I have REALLY FUCKED UP PRIORITIES MY DAMN SELF! LOL I told y'all I have DUMB BITCH issues too! Shit, we all do! My Sin… BILLS I hate, hate, paying them! Yuup I'm guilty as charged!

Now back to my regularly programmed Bitching!

Explain to me how you can be so terrified of your former "abuser" to the point where you keep your children out of school for an ENTIRE school year, however, you're brave enough, to leave your home to gamble, go out on dates (all while leaving the children all alone and or with a subpar baby sitter). I mean if you're so scared for your children's safety, that you can't enroll them in school, how is it you're not too afraid to leave them home "practically" all alone?

It's obvious that you're NOT SCARED for their safety, & or your own YOU DUMB BITCH! Remember, actions speak louder than words. YOU SURE AS HELL AREN'T CONCERNED WITH THEIR WELL BEING, I mean how can you be when it's been damn near a year since they've seen the inside of a classroom!?! No, you just have your priorities FUCKED UP YOU DUMB BITCH! You disgust me on so many different levels, that it's not even funny! You really are one of the WORSE kinds of DUMB BITCH! Yet, I have the strangest feeling that YOU think, YOU deserve to be MOTHER OF THE MOTHERFUCKING YEAR! I can't help but to laugh at you and your false sense of self-worth!

Explain to me, how you have money to get your hair done/cut, money to get high, money to get drunk, money to hit the clubs with, money to stay fly/fresh to death with, BUT you don't have any money to take care of your children? And I'm talking about the basics here; clothing, shoes, food, you know shit they require to LIVE a decent fucking life you moron! Oh, I know It's NOT that you don't have the money you DUMB BITCH it's that YOUR PRIORITIES are screwed the FUCK UP!! Get your fucking life together you DUMB BITCH!

Explain to me, how NONE of your bills are paid on time if at all, BUT you just bought a brand new pair of shoes? Explain to me how, your rent isn't paid on time if at all, you owe the IRS money, BUT you're planning on throwing your child the party of the year? So let me get this straight, your bills aren't paid, your rent isn't paid, you owe the IRS money, and yet you seem to think it's still a good idea and a good decision to go ahead and throw (your version of) the party of the year? LORD knows MTV would have surely laughed in your fucking face! YOUR PRIORITIES ARE SO SCREWED THE FUCK UP that it's not even funny! Get a grip YOU DUMB BITCH!

What all of YOU DUMB BITCHES with FUCKED UP ASS PRIORITIES need to do, Is JUST STOP and be FUCKING STILL! Sit back and re-evaluate your situation as a matter of fact, re-evaluate your fucking life! You would be much better off, and life wouldn't seem as fucked up as it does, IF YOU JUST GOT YOUR FUCKING PRIORITIES IN ORDER! Please people, get a grip and find a fucking clue. Because when the world looks at you, all we see, IS ANOTHER DUMB ASS BITCH!

I would say, go get it together and come join us in "The Diva Lane" but quite frankly you're a lame, and your presence isn't even wanted here! #LoserAlert

Chapter 7

DUMB BITCHES that fall victim to Domestic Violence

***PLEASE PROCEED WITH CAUTION!*

This topic is NO JOKING Matter! And let me start by first saying that I am PISSED the FUCK off about the media turning Rihanna into the poster-child for Domestic Violence and making Chris Brown out to be the fucking DEVIL! Now I'm NOT in any way shape or form condoning a man hitting on a woman for any fucking reason, but what I am saying is that Domestic Violence did not start with the 2 love struck young birds and it will NOT end with them, so GET THE FUCK OVER IT AMERICA!!

Now back to my regularly scheduled bitching!

Please answer this question for me, WHAT THE FUCK IS WRONG WITH YOU, THAT YOU WOULD CONTINUOUSLY ALLOW SOME DUMB FUCK BITCH ASS NIGGA TO WHIP ON YOUR FUCKING ASS? Are you some kind of fucktard? Now this doesn't apply to women who were struck once and got the fuck out, because you women are very smart and I commend you on your courage and your will to live, kudos to you! But for you DUMB BITCHES that stay, I barely feel fucking sorry for you. I damn near feel like your DUMB BITCH ASS deserves it! Why the fuck are you still there? Do you like it? What the fuck are you so afraid of? Because if you stay that DUMB MOTHERFUCKER is sure to fucking kill you, so to say you're afraid he'll kill you if you try to leave is just a bit redundant to me!

Fear is a crippling disease Ladies! And I know that some of you are afraid to leave because he may find you and whip your ass or find you and kill you, but what I don't get, is why the fuck aren't you afraid that he will come home pissed tonight and kill your DUMB BITCH ASS any fucking way? If you're going to die, you might as well die fighting!

I don't give a fuck if you have no money and or no place to go! I don't give a fuck if you have no plan, because you DON'T NEED a plan to get the fuck away from someone who is causing you bodily harm! You don't need an excuse, plan, or money to get away from some deranged fucktard! Let me clue your scary ass in on something, HE WILL NEVER EVER CHANGE! HE WILL NEVER EVER STOP BEATING ON YOU! HE DOESN'T MEAN IT WHEN HE SAYS HE'S SORRY! TRUE CHANGE COMES FROM WITHIN, NOT FROM SOMEONE ELSE PRAYING AND HOPING FOR CHANGE TO COME!

A woman beater is a LIAR therefore you CAN NOT trust ANYTHING he says! Get it?? Got it?? Good! I know that you are scared, and my heart breaks for you, it truly does in fact I pity you, because your fear is what has you in that situation and it is what's keeping you there! You have to STOP being afraid and get ready to fight! Get ready to take your fucking life back! The bullshit STOPS right here and right fucking now!

This is what I want you to do tonight before you go to bed, I want you to pray that God (Jehovah, Allah, Buddha) **whatever you call your one true God** to deliver you from this situation and this is the prayer that I want you to say;

Dear God, I am sick and tired of this FUCKTARD whipping on my ass (its okay to curse because the Lord knows your heart and he knows your sick and tired of this FUCKTARDS bullshit), and I'm scared out of my fucking mind! I don't have any money, and I have no place to go, BUT I have to get the fuck out of here! This burden is too much for my heart and soul to carry so I'm placing it in your hands. Tomorrow when I wake up I'm getting the FUCK out of here and placing my life and destiny on your shoulders so that you may carry this weight for me! I have nothing left and nothing to lose, I pray that I make it out safely but if something should go terribly wrong, I pray that my life and death will be an inspiration for others to get out before it is too late (because let's face it.. unfortunately as statistics would have it some of you will die)! I pray that if I die my death can save the life of another. Dear GOD I hope that you have heard my prayer this evening, because today is the day, I've decided to take my life back! I pray that you give me strength, courage, and wisdom to make it through! You are MY rock, MY everything, MY shelter in the storm, and in YOU ALONE I TRUST! Amen!

The next day all you have to do is fulfill your end of the bargain and GET THE FUCK OUT! God did NOT bless you with life to watch that DUMB FUCKTARD beat you down! He wants more and better for you, but you have to want it for yourself! When you walk out of that house, apartment, or situation the next day, BITCH RUN LIKE HELL AND DON'T stop until you can't run anymore! Stop somebody anybody and ask for help. God will place an angel in your path to aid you, but you have to have FAITH that he will save you and deliver you from that fucked up ass situation! Shit you don't have control of your life or freedom anymore, so all you have is your FAITH! Hold on to it, believe in it, and it will set you free!

HERE IS A TOLL FREE HOTLINE FOR SAFE HORIZONS & A LINK TO THEIR WEBSITE;
1.800.621.4673

http://www.safehorizon.org/

When you reach somewhere safe, the home of a friend, family member, a neighbor, domestic violence safe house, church, or even the home of a stranger, better yet when you reach THE POLICE STATION, call Safe Horizons, and tell them your situation. I don't care where you are or what you have, THEY WILL GET YOU THE FUCK AWAY FROM THAT MONSTER!!

** I will say this.. if it is possible for you to document your abuse do so.. Have someone you trust take pictures, write it in a diary, buy a laptop and store it in a safe place and take pictures of your scars, wounds, black eyes with your web cam.. But try your best to document all forms of abuse!

I know that starting over can be scary for some of you, and may damn near seem impossible, but NOTHING is impossible when you have faith! I've witnessed women over come Domestic Abuse and I know that YOU can overcome it too! Take Back Your Life! TODAY IS THE DAY!!

And when you get away from that deranged DUMB BITCH motherfucker, Bitch, PLEASE take some sort of self-defense class, learn Karate, or learn how to bust a cap in a motherfucker's ass effectively! SHOOT TO KILL YOU DUMB BITCH!

"For what shall it profit a man, if he shall gain the whole world, and lose his own soul"? King James Bible

Chapter 8

Ungrateful ass MEN!

(Oh you thought that men were excluded from being DUMB ASS BITCHES)?
NOT!

UNGRATEFUL ASS MEN, yeah ya'll know the type. And I'm about to put all their little UNGRATEFUL ASSES on motherfucking BLAST 5.4.3.2.1 here it come!

Let me start by saying, I can't stand you UNGRATEFUL FUCKTARDS! You walk around acting like you are God's gift to women, when ALL YOU REALLY ARE IS A FUCKING BURDEN! Your woman puts up with you, because she LOVES YOU! NOT because she can't find another man! Let me rephrase, NOT because she can't find a man! Because let's face it, WE ALL KNOW THAT YOU ARE NO MAN! JUST A PATHETIC EXCUSE FOR ONE! What you need to do, is a get a grip, and find a fucking clue! You're a fucking loser and a disgrace to all REAL MEN! You want to know why your woman doesn't want to fuck you, much less suck your nasty ass dick? Because YOU FUCKING DISGUST HER, that's why! Every time she looks at you, all she wants to do is VOMIT! Being broke, unemployed, and a basic waste of space is SO NOT CUTE, you dumb motherfucker! Just the fucking sight of you makes her want to slap the fucking shit out of you! YOU ARE DEAD FUCKING WEIGHT! Know that NOW, and I mean RIGHT NOW!

And for all of you motherfuckers that go to jail and complain about how your woman up and left you and she didn't ride with you, this is WHY! BECAUSE the DUMB BITCH motherfucker that came before you left a DISGUSTING TASTE IN HER MOUTH!! She did ALL OF THAT FUCKING TIME WITH HIM!!! And for what, so he could turn around and FUCK a 16 YEAR OLD!?! Yeah, he thought she wouldn't find out, hehehe! BUT SHE DID AND SHE WHIPPED HIS MOTHERFUCKING ASS WITH AN EXTENSION CHORD, like a run a way slave! That's right, she BEAT THAT MOTHERFUCKER like he stole something! (True Story, what up Co-D) HAHAHA, serves his DUMB BITCH ASS right! Stupid Ungrateful ass Motherfucker!!

ALL YOU UNGRATEFUL BASTARDS BETTER TAKE HEED TO WHAT I'M SAYING...

1. YOU ARE *NOT* GOD'S GIFT TO WOMEN
2. YOU *ARE* A BURDEN
3. YOUR WOMAN (*IF SHE IS SMART*) WILL LEAVE YOU &
4. ***NO REAL WOMAN WILL EVER TOLERATE YOUR SORRY ASS!***

When your woman comes home tonight, have the house cleaned, and dinner cooked, LMAO because face it, YOU'RE THE BITCH IN THIS RELATIONSHIP!! You Dumb Ungrateful Motherfucker!

Chapter 9

Self-Hating DUMB BITCHES

Let me start by saying, SELF-Hate and LOW SELF-Esteem are killers you DUMB BITCH!

Now, back to my regularly scheduled bitching!

Look here you DUMB BITCH, let me clue your ass in on something, the only reason your black ass wants a white/light baby is because you hate your fucking self and because you have LOW Self-Esteem! If you are so fucking concerned about what complexion your baby is going to be or how nappy their hair is going to be, THEN DON'T FUCKING REPRODUCE! Because GOD forbid you don't have the little white/light baby you want all you're going to do is teach that child how to hate themselves the way that you hate YOU! You are a pathetic disgrace to our race! BLACK IS BEAUTIFUL! It always has been and it always will be, despite what your ignorant ass thinks!

Stop looking at your baby when he/she turns 2 and wondering what happened to the straight hair he/she was born with! Better yet stop telling people I don't know what happened, he/she was born with a head full of straight/curly hair! I will tell you what the fuck happened, NATURE YOU DUMB BITCH! NATURE HAPPENED! Your placenta relaxed/permed the baby's hair you moron! THAT'S WHY your baby was born with curly/straight hair! NOT because your Grandma's Best Friends Uncle was Native American you SELF-Hating DUMB BITCH! Not because your, Great-great-great-great Uncle was half-fucking white! So just stop it you DUMB BITCH! Know for a FACT and without a doubt, that while your child "may" pickup a recessive gene and come out lighter than expected or with hair that isn't as coarse as yours, that the chances of your baby coming out just like you and or his/her father IS GREATER! Accept it and deal with it! As a matter of fact what you need to be most concerned with, is that the baby doesn't turn out to be an IGNORANT SELF-HATING FUCKTARD LIKE YOU!

Answer me this, when did light skin start to equal cute? I mean it's 2010, clearly your ignorant ass must have noticed by now, that there are quite a few ugly light skinned motherfuckers running around here! Answer me this, when did dark skin start to equal ugly? I mean it's 2010, clearly your ignorant ass must have noticed by now, that, there are more than a little bit of beautiful, chocolate, sexy motherfuckers running around! Or are you just that fucking ignorant?

The color of your skin and your children's skin isn't the problem. What's going on in that small pea sized brain of yours is! The fact that its 2010 and you're still as ignorant as ever, that's a problem! NOT the color of your child's skin or the texture of their hair!

I hate DUMB BITCHES that treat or favor their light skinned children over the dark ones! It's NOT the child's fault that the color of his/her skin isn't to your liking you DUMB BITCH! Think back, when did it start? Where does this self-hate come from? When did you first realize you suffered from low self-esteem? Or have you not realized that not only is your self-esteem fucked up, but you hate yourself as well you ignorant DUMB BITCH?

Just know this, if YOU don't love yourself, how can you ever expect anyone else to love you? And if you don't like what you see when you look in the mirror, what do you think the world sees when they look at you?

Chapter 10

My Two Cents on DUMB BITCHES who INSIST on Having "Keep a Nigga" Babies

Okay ya'll, I know that there are quite a few DUMB BITCH scenarios that get under my skin, and I've bitched about some of them already. But at the tip top of that list are all you DUMB BITCHES that keep trying to lock a Nigga down or force him to be a part of your pathetic lives by having what I so kindly refer to as a "Keep a Nigga Baby"!

**Nigga: MAN and NOT of any particular; race, creed, or nationality.

Listen here you DUMB BITCH, what you need to do is get a grip and find a fucking clue! Because a baby isn't keeping any Nigga around, never has and never will! Stop pushing out those little bastards if you don't want them! Because if the Daddy didn't want them when your ass got knocked up, he sure as hell isn't going to want them when your ass drops!

So stop trying to keep a Nigga in your life by having his baby! All you're doing is bringing another fatherless Bastard into this world, like we don't already have enough of those! I keep saying it, and I'm going to keep saying it until you DUMB BITCHES get it through your thick fucking air filled skulls, Low Self-Esteem is a Killer, seek help bitch!

Work on you before you try to work some psychological bull shit on him. At the end of the day all you are to him and everyone who knows you is a DUMB BITCH!

And, another thing, babies are NOT a come up you DUMB BITCH! STOP having babies that you don't want for monetary gain. Not only is it disgusting, but it makes you the worst kind of whore! What is your kid going to think when he or she grows up to find out, that Mommy got pregnant by the TURKEY BASTER! How long do you think you'll be able to keep that little secret from him or her?

Especially when there is a DUMB BITCH hater like me on the loose, ready and willing to expose your DUMB BITCH ass!

STOP, having babies with married men! HE is not going to leave his wife just because your DUMB BITCH ASS went and got knocked up! He'll pay someone to kill your stupid ass first. Or better yet, he and his WIFE will prove you to be an unfit mother, take your baby, and raise it as their own! But you're such a DUMB BITCH that, you haven't even placed that much thought into your wack ass idea!

You know what really pisses me off about you DUMB BITCHES, is that you really have the nerve to get mad at the man for not wanting you and your baby, when he made it MORE than clear that he didn't want either of you BEFORE you even had the damn baby! What the fuck made you think that would change? Did you really think that he would come around, tell you he loves you, and try to win the father of the year award? LMAO, you did, didn't you? Lord have mercy, you are dumber than you look!

So now what do you do, your plan hasn't worked, he isn't coming around, he isn't calling, he's changed his number because he doesn't want you calling him, so what do you do? I know, you try and get some child support out of him, because he's going to pay and be a father to your little bastard by hook or crook, isn't he? But wait, then you realize, if you take him to court he may get visitation rights as well, and you don't want that do you? No, what you want is for him to visit you! So now what do you do? NOTHING just sit there in your fucking roach infested rat whole with another fatherless bastard you DUMB BITCH!

In case you didn't hear me before, let me say this again, a baby, ain't keeping no Nigga around! I mean shit at least he was fucking your desperate ass once upon a time, now you can't even get the dick anymore. See where your ignorance and denial got you, NOTHING! It got you absolutely nothing! You really are pathetic you really are a DUMB BITCH in ever essence of the term.

Chapter 11

DUMB BITCHES that insist on fucking for FREE

I am sick and tired of all you DUMB ASS BITCHES who stay fucking these Niggas for FREE! Stop letting Niggas come to your crib, eat your food, smoke your weed, drink your liquor, and use your pussy for his own selfish reasons, (because I know the Nigga doesn't care if you get yours) and leave without breaking you off! Then you want to call your friends and borrow money that, that Nigga OWE YOU!

Let me clue your DUMB ASS in on something, when you call your friends, do you know what they are saying about you? "DAMN YOU A DUMB ASS BITCH"! If you're going to fuck for free, then fuck yourself you DUMB BITCH!!

What you need to do is learn to peep game from these lame as motherfuckers! Sex does not equal love, shit, it doesn't even equal like!

So, in this chapter I have decided to do you poor lost sheep a favor. I'm going to teach you how to peep game, from these lame ass Niggas/Predators.

First off ladies, before I go any further let me first say for this to work, you have to know your worth!

Now some of us are worth a lot, and some of you aren't really worth shit. Whatever it is, Know YOUR worth.

As a guide, if you're a Chapter 1 type of DUMB BITCH, your worth is currently 0, if you're a Chapter 10 type of DUMB BITCH, your worth is also currently 0, because you're just a basic run of the mill LOSER if you're worth is currently valued at 0, please work on yourself first. Then proceed reading, because frankly no matter what you say or do, all you're currently worth is getting fucked for free, you DUMB BITCH!

Now, back to the lesson for today; How to peep game!

1. Watch out for lame ass game.

    a) If the 1st thing a dude tells you after you meet is how he's always busy because he stays on his grind or because he has to watch his kids, this means; BITCH I AIN'T GOT NO TIME FOR YOU!

    b) If he likes to spend (what you consider) way too much time talking about all the bills he has to pay, this mean; BITCH DON'T ASK ME FOR NOTHING BECAUSE I'M A CHEAP FUCK!

    c) If he's always telling you some wild ass story about his friend and how he degrades women in any way, shape, or form, this means; BITCH I WOULD TELL YOU THAT I'M THE ASSHOLE THAT DID ALL OF THOSE THINGS BUT I CAN'T BE HONEST WITH YOU BECAUSE I'M STILL TRYING TO FUCK YOU!

Ladies you have to learn how to read between the lines! Stop running your damn mouth so much and let him speak. A man will let you know his intentions and what kind of dude he is, if you just let him do the talking. Learn how to peep LAME ASS GAME!

And don't ever fuck a Nigga because you "THINK" that after you fuck him, he will start spending that cash! If he didn't spend it in an attempt to get the ass, he sure as hell isn't going to spend it after he gets it! GET IT? GOT IT? GOOD!

2. Bitch, if you don't have anything, i.e. an education, your own place, your own car, SOMETHING, ANYTHING that is YOURS, stop talking about what a Nigga has to have to fuck with you.

    a) <u>**A NIGGA THAT HAS WANTS A BITCH THAT HAS**</u>! We are in a recession no one is looking for a delusional DUMB ASS BITCH that's looking to be carried! (Besides, if you have nothing then you're either a Chapter 1 or Chapter 10 type of DUMB BITCH, and I already told you that this section DOES NOT APPLY TO YOU, because you're current worth is 0)

3. Bitch, if you have your own, i.e. education, place, car, career, STOP dealing with LAME DUMB BITCH NIGGAS that don't have shit!

   a) You can do better and you deserve better.
   b) All a DUMB BITCH HATIN ASS NIGGA is going to do is try to take you down and make you feel like shit, because you have your shit together!
   c) What you need to do is find a MAN worthy of YOU!
   d) STOP SETTLING!

So, today's lesson is;

1. Stop fucking for free
2. Know your worth
3. Stop settling

Get it? Got it? Good!

Chapter 12

He is your son/brother/cousin/baby-daddy/friend NOT YOUR MAN

I hate DUMB BITCH mothers, sisters, cousins, baby-mamas, and friends who act like their son, brother, cousin, baby-daddy, or friend is their Man!

Listen up DUMB ASS BITCHES, you are not the one who is fucking him, you are not the one he comes home too, so STOP fucking acting like he is!

Get your own fucking man, stop calling him every fucking second begging and shit! Call that Nigga that's fucking you, call that Nigga that's smoking up your weed for free.

If you have an array of children, brothers, sisters, cousins, or baby-daddies call one of their fucking asses instead! If you only have one child etc., TOUGH FUCKING TITTY says the kitty, because you need to become independent!

STOP leaning on your son, brother etc like he doesn't have a fucking life of his own!

Is it that you don't care he has, HIS OWN CHILD/REN to care for, HIS OWN HOME to maintain, a woman/wife to take care of? If so then that's a clear indication that, you are nothing more than a DUMB SELFISH BITCH! Stop trying to turn him into all of the men that left you! It is NOT his fault that you are lonely, miserable, and pathetic! It's not his fault that the men in your life, feel that you have absolutely no worth and or value, and treat you like a piece of fucking trash! I mean you're the DUMB BITCH that keeps fucking on them, allowing them to come over to your house, smoke your weed and get their dicks sucked for free, NOT your son/brother etc. fault, so why should it be his concern that you need something done? Or that you need to go somewhere? Or that you need $20.00 with your crack head begging ass!

You fucking disgust me! Get your fucking life together you DUMB BITCH! He is your son/brother, etc. NOT your man! When are you going to get that through your big fucking air filled skull! Know what you are? A fucking loser, and a disgrace to all REAL WOMEN like me, living life "Fierce, Focused, & FABULOUSLY"! ** Now in the rare instance that you are fucking him; well 1 that makes you nasty, 2 that makes you his Sideline Hoe, and 3 that means you still don't matter and you're still a DUMB ASS BITCH! HA, no exceptions here Heifer!

In any event, at the end of the day, whether someone else has already told you or not, all you are is a lonely, pathetic, DUMB ASS BITCH who is getting fucked for free!

Chapter 13

DUMB BITCHES that "THINK" they're hot when they're NOT

Okay, so let's get down to business! Let's talk about all of these DUMB BITCHES running around town thinking they're hot when they're NOT!

You know the kind, she's always bragging about who she knows, and where she goes. Then you go out with the DUMB BITCH, just to find out, not only is she a NOBODY, but NOBODY knows her! LMFAO, you go out with her and she realizes what a real HOT bitch really looks like because your flow is UNSTOPPABLE! LMAO, I know ya'll know the type!

This Bitch always bragging about what party she's at, what party she's going to, who knows her, and how she can get into any venue that she goes to. But, when you get to the venue if you weren't there with her, her ass would have been stuck outside at the door! LMAO, ya'll know the type.

She tells you about her man, and how much he loves her, and when she introduces the two of you he brushes right past her to get to you, LMAO, ya'll know the type. Then when you ask him, "Why he's disrespecting his woman like that"? He says, "What woman"? "I don't have a woman, I'm single"! LMAO! And when you look at her she's holding her head down like a wounded dog! LMFAO, ya'll know the type! On the way home, she confesses, "Well we're not together, together" NO BITCH you're just NOT together, LMFAO, ya'll know the type!

Well I wish these DUMB BITCHES would just get it the fuck together, because LORD HAVE MERCY do they look wack! Bitch you're not hot, you never have been, and you never will be!

When will they learn, that their false sense of self will only get them embarrassed more times than NOT? So, please, just STOP!

Case and Point

I know of this DUMB BITCH that is always in the club, frontin and stuntin, posing for flicks and she is UGLY as SHIT (word on the street is Niggas on the club scene refer to her as "Tranny" behind her back)! LMMFAO because she swears up & down that they're her "friends". This particular Dumb Bitch is dumb for more reasons than 1! And can probably relate to more than 1 chapter in this self-help guide! #FACT

This bitch is so fucking delusional that she often refers to herself as a DIVA! Bitch, are you serious?

You're NOT a DIVA! You're just an UGLY, POOR CHOICE IN MEN, BALD HEADED/BAD WEAVE HAVING: DUMB, DELUSIONAL ASS BITCH that thinks she's hot, when she's REALLY NOT!

Get it? Got it? GOOD!

Chapter 14

Act your age you DUMB BITCH
Feigning a mid-life crisis isn't Cute

I hate DUMB BITCHES in their late thirties and forties that still don't have their shit together!

Bitch, life is not a fucking dress rehearsal! You don't get a fucking do-over! Stop trying to live vicariously through your fucking child/ren and get your shit together, because when the world looks at you all we see is another DUMB BUM ASS BITCH! Sound familiar?

I can't stand these old heifers forty plus, that walk around behaving like school girls!

I don't want to hear, well I don't feel old. Bitch, no one asked you how you felt, and this isn't about how you feel, this is about what you are! And what you are, is OLD! So please stop acting like you're not!

Stop wearing your teenage daughters clothing, stop getting tattoos, stop talking about what clubs are poppin, and what dudes you just met! Grow the fuck up you DUMB SIMPLE BITCH! You look fucking pathetic!

The only reason these young men are paying you any attention is because they know you're DESPERATE and that you will pretty much do anything in an attempt (a sad one) to keep their attention on you! I.e. Buy them things, loan them your car, cook for them (and wrap it up for him to take home, because he is not about to sit and have dinner with your old hag looking ass), finance him his own car, and the list goes on. You know exactly what the fuck you do, you pathetic DUMB BITCH!

What are you afraid of? Oh I know; you know a man your age doesn't want you either. He either wants something young and tender or a woman of a certain age who has embraced her maturity and is ready to move on to the next chapter of her life. He doesn't want some old heifer in her forties that behaves as if she were in her twenties you DUMB BITCH!

In the end all you're doing is short changing yourself!

Please do us all a favor, get a grip and find a fucking clue! Because at the end of the day a woman in her forties that behaves as if she were in her twenties, is just sad and pathetic!

GROW UP YOU DUMB BITCH!

Chapter 15

DUMB BITCHES that would much rather take care of a man instead of their child/ren

Okay, these particular DUMB BITCHES get under MY FUCKING skin and on my DAMN NERVES too!

I am sick and fucking tired of DUMB BITCHES that would much rather take care of some good for nothing LAZY ASS Nigga, than herself or her fucking children! BITCH, get your fucking life in order and your priorities straight!

Why would you spend HUNDREDS or THOUSANDS of dollars on a man that isn't YOURS when you have YOURSELF and YOUR CHILDREN to care for? What kind of FUCKTARD are you? You haven't paid any of your fucking bills, but you bought your "Boo" some new sneakers! You haven't paid YOUR rent, but you paid your "Boo's" car note and insurance (because how was he gone get to the club to mack on some more DUMB ASS BITCHES like you)!

You are so fucking pathetic and desperate that it's a damn shame! You can't take your kid to a movie, because you had to pay your "Boo's" cell phone bill! You have no food in your house, but he's got money to pop bottles at the club tonight! YOU'RE ONE OF THE WORSE KINDS OF DUMB BITCHES! Please know that's a FACT and its BEYOND A REASONABLE DOUBT! Oh, and please believe the list of DUMB BITCH shit you do for your "Boo" goes on, and on, and on!

Here's a list of must have's before you even think you have enough to give to some lazy ass Nigga!

1. All of your bills must be paid
2. Your refrigerator must be stocked to the top at all times with top of the line brand items

3. All of your children's needs AND wants must've been met
4. You must have already taken your monthly spa day
5. You must have purchased at least one impulse item &
6. You must have already put money into your savings account, IRA, and your child/ren's college fund(s)

Now unless you have placed a check next to every item on my list, and I know damn well you haven't you have no spare change to give that motherfucker!

Take care of yourself and your children first! That is your responsibility! He has a Mama, let him call her ass!

Let me clue your DUMB BITCH ASS in on something, a man that truly cares for you, WOULD NEVER TAKE FOOD OUT OF YOUR MOUTH OR THE MOUTH'S OF YOUR CHILDREN! A man that truly cares for you, will be MORE interested in putting FOOD into your mouth and the mouths of your children! Your "Boo" DOESN'T GIVE A FUCK ABOUT YOUR DUMB BITCH ASS! He is using you and manipulating you because YOU ARE WEAK! And, more importantly he knows that YOU ARE JUST THAT FUCKING DESPERATE! He laughs at you behind your back, he talks about you behind your back, and secretly YOU DISGUST HIM! He will never WIFE you because 1. HE'S NOT A REAL MAN and 2. A DUMB BITCH is NEVER EVER viewed as WIFE MATERIAL!

Get YOUR fucking priorities straight YOU DUMB BITCH! Because when a man sees that you value YOURSELF and YOUR CHILDREN above HIM, he will know that he will have to value you and them the same!

You should want a man that enhances YOU! NOT one that takes from you! But, because YOU'RE A DUMB BITCH you don't get that! You actually think that LAZY ASS MAN LOVES YOU! But, I guess that's what separates DUMB ASS BITCHES like YOU from REAL ASS BITCHES like ME!

Chapter 16

They're either Haters or Band Wagon Jumpers

Is it me, or is every DUMB BITCH you encounter these days a "Band Wagon Jumper" or a "Hater"? I know it can't be just me!

HATERS

Okay, so basically I fucking hate "Haters"! I hate people that try their very best to shoot down the dreams and hopes of others, just because they have none. You know the type, no matter how good or great your idea may be they just have to shit on it! No matter how good your business plan may be, they just have to give you all of the reasons why their DUMB BITCH ASS doesn't think it will work. I fucking HATE HATERS!

Listen here you DUMB BITCH, just because your pathetic life is headed nowhere fast doesn't mean that you should hate on and try to shit on your friends! Whose life contrary to your stupid fucking beliefs is headed somewhere! What you should do is use that Bad Bitch as motivation to get your life in order and your shit together! Ask that Bad Bitch for some advice or study her and take notes. You don't have to be a DUMB HATIN ASS BITCH, you can be a Bad Bitch too!

First you have to accept the fact, that you're not just a DUMB BITCH, but you're a DUMB HATIN ASS BITCH too! Once you've accepted it and are ready to move past it, you will see that you can be something too! You can dream and have aspirations of being something or doing something great with your life too! And watch as they begin to manifest themselves into your waking life!

You weren't born a DUMB BITCH you just became one by default. So see DUMB BITCHES, there's hope for you after all!

Band Wagon Jumpers

DUMB BITCHES that insist on jumping on your band wagon, oh you know the kind! Anything you do, either they've done it, were just about to do it, or now they want to do it too!

I hate those unoriginal DUMB ASS BITCHES!

Bitch, get a fucking mind of your own and stop trying to use mine!

It's almost like they've never had one original fucking thought! I hate those BITCHES! You go into a store and buy something, all of a sudden they have to have the same damn thing, or they wait a few days and pop up at your crib with the same damn shirt/pants/hat/glasses/shoes/sneakers that they witnessed you purchase on! And what makes it worse? That's right, when they say, "Oh you have this"? "Girl I forgot you bought this"! Bitch, no the fuck you didn't! Or they see you rocking your new hairdo and what do they say? Oh I used to have my hair cut like that too, but I decided to let it grow out. Or I was just about to get that haircut too! Bitch NO the fuck you weren't!

Sometimes I wonder what'll happen to those DUMB BITCHES if I just up and decide to pull a disappearing act. Would they run around like chickens with their little fucking heads cut off? LMMFAO at the thought… probably!

Bitch stop trying to be like me and figure out who the fuck you are!

I hate those DUMB BITCHES!

Oh I did that. Oh I was about to do that. Oh I think I'm going to do that too!

No BITCH, don't! Just Stop, be still, and get your shit together! Because no matter how hard you try, you can NEVER EVER and will NEVER EVER BE ME!

At the end of the day, know that it doesn't matter, whether you're a "Hater" and or a "Band Wagon Jumper" playing either position makes you a DUMB BITCH!

Chapter 17

DUMB BITCHES The Recession and The "American" Dream

Everyone is pissed and broke behind this recession. Everyone is looking to blame this catastrophe on someone; *President Bush, Illegal Immigrants, The Big Banks, Wall St., Predatory Lending*, I mean people have entire lists of other people, businesses, politicians, and reasons as to what caused this "recession". Which quite frankly is starting to resemble a fucking "great depression" to me, YET NO ONE HAS STATED THE OBVIOUS, SO, PLEASE ALLOW ME.

THE REAL CULPRIT, the ones that are truly to blame, are The DUMB BITCHES of AMERICA!

That's right, I said it, DUMB BITCHES caused the recession!

It's said that ignorance is bliss. Well outside of it being blissful, apparently it is also detrimental TO AN ENTIRE FUCKING NATION!

Every thing that is happening to our country and economy is the direct result of a DUMB BITCH and her/his fucked up decision making! They're the first to say, "I was a victim of predatory lending, and now I'm homeless" NO you DUMB BITCH, you are a victim of ignorance! NOT predatory lending! Yeah Bush was a whack ass President, probably one of the worst in history, however it is NOT HIS FAULT, Wall St.'s fault, or any other politicians, or Big Banks fault that you are a DUMB, IGNORANT, and IRRESPONSIBLE ASS BITCH!

Everyone wants a piece of the "American Dream" called HOME OWNERSHIP. Now while there is essentially nothing wrong with wanting to own a home, know RIGHT NOW that home ownership is NOT FOR EVERYONE.

I am going to make a list and if you can identify with any of the choices on this list you are a DUMB BITCH and are partially responsible for our economy being in the fucked up ass state that it is currently in.

The List

1. If you were in Landlord/Tenant COURT for NON-PAYMENT of rent (YOU ARE NOT READY TO OWN A HOME).

2. If you make $30,000 or less, & constantly complain about paying your $800-$1300 rent (YOU ARE NOT READY TO OWN A HOME).

3. If you let some dumb motherfucker with an even smaller I.Q. and less of an education than you, convince you that not only are you ready to own a home but can afford to pay a $3500 + mortgage, when you are currently struggling to pay your rent (ranges above) (YOU ARE NOT READY TO OWN A HOME).

4. If you are on welfare and view this as a career (YOU ARE NOT READY TO OWN A HOME).

5. If keeping your kids and woman/man fly/fresh is more important to you (keeping up with the Jones's) than paying your bills (YOU ARE NOT READY TO OWN A HOME).

6. If your cell phone bill is paid, you have on a fresh new outfit and you're headed out the door on your way to your favorite club/bar, BUT your rent ISN'T paid (YOU ARE NOT READY TO OWN A HOME).

7. If you still have to ask, "How do I find out my credit score"? (YOU ARE NOT READY TO OWN A HOME).

8. If you're credit score is less that 650, but yet and still "you think" you should qualify for 100% financing, and are confused when you don't get it (YOU ARE NOT READY TO OWN A HOME).

9. If you have attended credit counseling and or have completed some sort of credit counseling program, but your credit is still fucked up (YOU ARE NOT READY TO OWN A HOME).

10. If AFTER reading this, all you can say is, What the Fuck is a credit score? (THEN TRUST AND BELIEVE ME WHEN I TELL YOU, THAT NOT ONLY ARE YOU NOT READY BUT YOU WILL NEVER BE READY TO OWN A HOME)!

My 7 year old knows what the fuck a credit score is, you ignorant bitch!

Well that's all I have to say about that, any questions?

Chapter 18

Ode to Winter

Displaced anger is NOT CUTE Your "Man" is a Liar and a Cheat Boo!

Okay let's get serious for one minute ladies, because for the life of me I can't understand the levels of disrespect you are willing to accept and or stand for, all for the sake of saying "I have a man". First off, there's a real difference between a man, a boy, and a dog. Please be aware of which it is you have! If your "Man" comes in and out all hours of the day and night, chances are what you really have is a "dog" and not a "Man". If you have irrefutable proof that your "Man" is cheating, again chances are what you have is a "dog" and not a "Man". And if a "Man" isn't worthy of the title "Man" then why are you bestowing it upon him you DUMB BITCH?!?

What the fuck is wrong with you? How can you let a man tell you a bullshit as lie, and after the proof given to you, I know it could've ONLY been bullshit, to pacify you? I mean, I really have to LOL at any BITCH dumb enough to still want to call a Nigga who's running all up and around town fucking everything in sight but them, their fucking man!

UNBELIEVEABLE! Bitch please check on your self-esteem because surely it is MISSING! My suggestion is you call your local police station and put an APB out on it STAT! You're a LOSER and the worse kind of DUMB BITCH because you're suffering from DISPLACED ANGER issues! You're mad at the wrong person you FUCKTARD!

I'm a Bitch with too much sass a REAL Five Star Bitch with class and I REFUSE to let some LOOSE DICK NIGGA make a fool out of me! If you don't respect yourself how the fuck can you expect a man to respect you?

Everything starts with SELF! Blame yourself, because you only have you to blame! If you accept a cheater to be a good enough "Man" for you, that is all you will ever have, and frankly all that your DUMB BITCH ASS deserves, and or will ever get because when you accept and expect BULLSHIT that's really all you should ever expect to get!

Now if your man always needs and wants, and expects you to always provide, chances are what you really have is a "boy" and not a "Man". The only person you should constantly have to provide for is your child and or children! A grown ass man should be able to provide for himself! Why are you calling him a "Man" when it's obvious that he is anything but that!?! Ask yourself why? Why am I this desperate? When did I become so desperate? When did the phrase "I have a man" begin to outweigh everything else in my life? When did the phrase "I have a man" start to matter more than me? What you need to do is reevaluate your entire situation! Aren't your children enough responsibility? Send that "boy" home to his Mama if what he still requires is a provider/caregiver and not a woman/partner! This way you're open to receiving and accepting the love and admiration of a real "Man" and not just one that wants you because of what you can do and or provide for him.

I know that letting go is hard to do ladies, but trust me when I tell you, YOU WILL THANK ME when you do, and sometimes the hardest thing to do is the only thing left to do!

Chapter 19

Epilogue

THE GRAND FINALE!
IN THE END…. Remember this…

Be strong not weak. Be brave not fearful. Be you not me. Be the best that you can possibly be. And always have FAITH that no matter how dark today was, tomorrows another day, and there's always the chance for a brighter day!

Live; like today is your last day. Love; like you've never been hurt before. Laugh; because laughter is the song of the soul.

Kisses Bitches,

MsSoSick

***DISCLAIMER

The events, topics, scenarios, situations, and Dumb Bitches depicted in this book have either been taken from my personal life, the lives of friends, family, acquaintances, fans, supporters, strangers, enemies, and or foes alike. If you have been offended by the comments in this book, I would apologize but honestly these are MY OPINIONS (which I am more than entitled to)! <u>As these events, topics, scenarios, and situations are not statistically factual and I have named no names, locations, & or particular incidents (I really just don't give a fuck if you're offended) I am NOT LIABLE in any form or fashion.</u> Be happy that your mistakes were able to inspire me in some way and can now help another man or woman grow! EACH one, TEACH one!

www.ingramcontent.com/pod-product-compliance
Ingram Content Group UK Ltd.
Pitfield, Milton Keynes, MK11 3LW, UK
UKHW041959230426
12048UKWH00008B/415